take it apart

CAR

By Chris Oxlade

Illustrated by Mike Grey

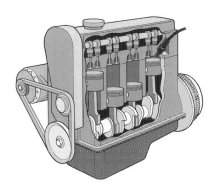

Thameside Press

Distributed in the United States by
Smart Apple Media
1980 Lookout Drive
North Mankato, MN 56003

Text copyright © Chris Oxlade
Illustrator copyright © Mike Grey

ISBN 1-930643-94-2

Library of Congress Control Number 2002 141348

Editor: Jilly MacLeod
Designer: Guy Callaby
Illustrator: Mike Grey
Consultants: Elizabeth Atkinson and Robin Kerrod

Printed by South China Printing Co. Ltd., Hong Kong

Inside this Book

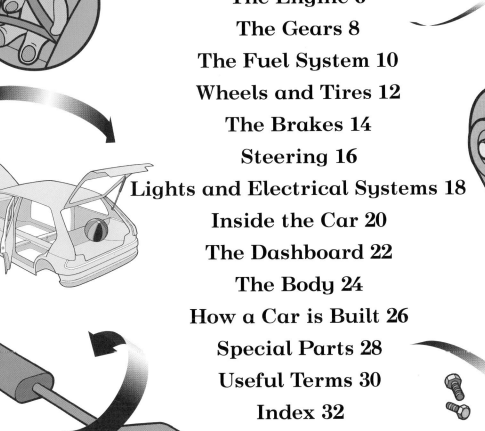

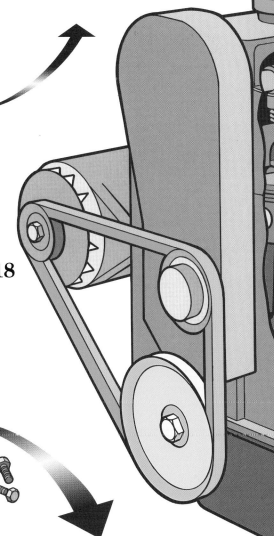

Take a Car Apart

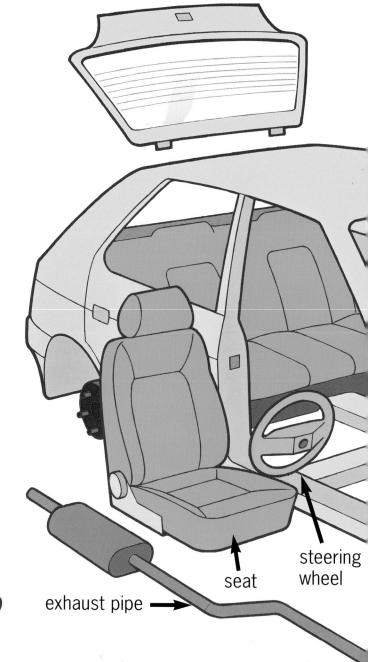

⊜ A car is made up of thousands of parts, big and small.

⊜ The parts are made of different materials such as metal, plastic, rubber, glass, and fabric. Sometimes leather and wood are used as well.

⊜ All the parts are put together in a car factory.

⊜ This book shows you the main parts of a car and how they all fit together.

exhaust pipe ⟶

seat

steering wheel

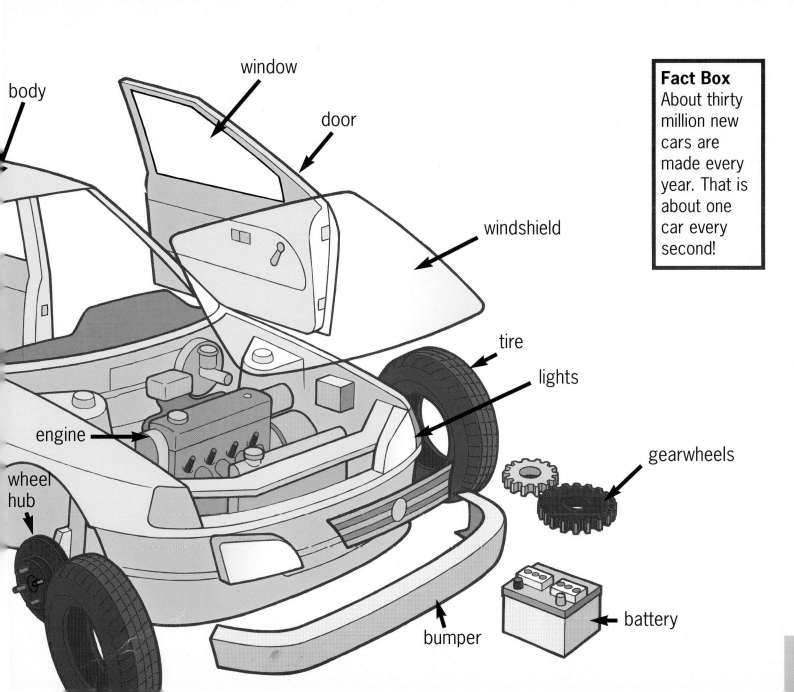

body

window

door

windshield

tire

lights

engine

wheel hub

gearwheels

bumper

battery

The Engine

- The engine makes the car move.

- Inside the engine are chambers called cylinders. Inside each cylinder is a piston, which moves up and down.

- Fuel, such as gas, is burned inside the cylinders to make the engine work.

- The driver presses the gas pedal with his or her foot to make the engine—and the car—go faster.

Spark plug
Spark plugs inside the engine make a spark, like a tiny flash of lightning, when electricity is passed through them.

spark

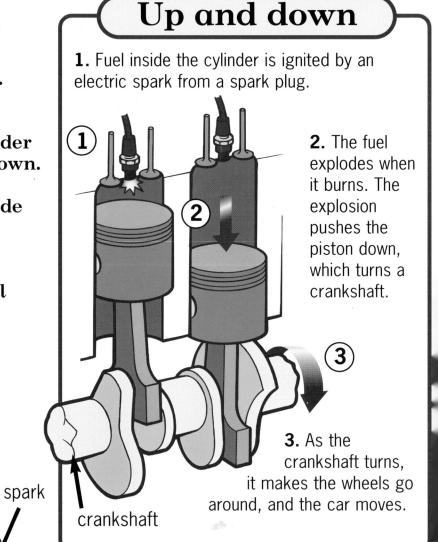

Up and down

1. Fuel inside the cylinder is ignited by an electric spark from a spark plug.

2. The fuel explodes when it burns. The explosion pushes the piston down, which turns a crankshaft.

3. As the crankshaft turns, it makes the wheels go around, and the car moves.

crankshaft

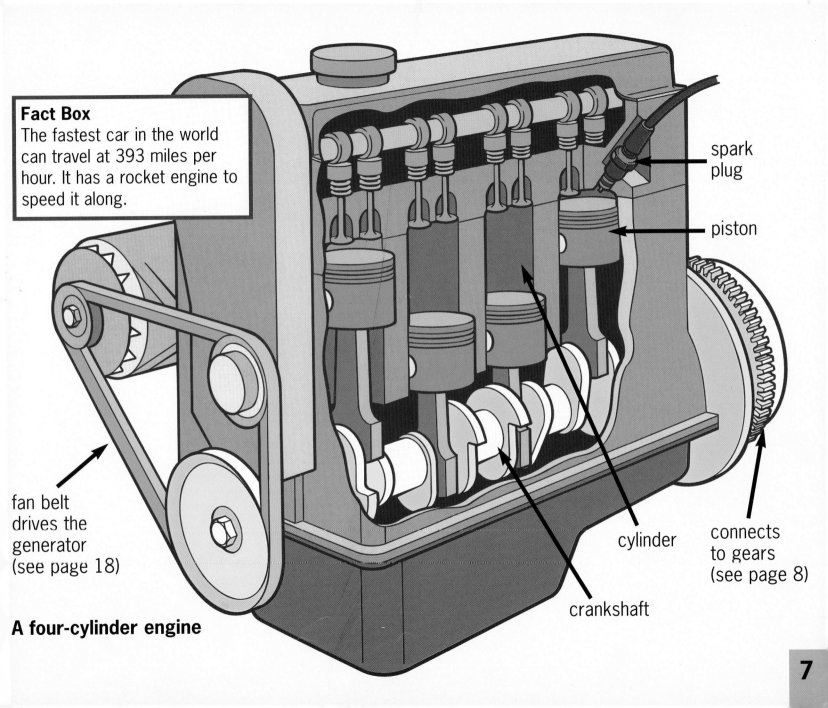

Fact Box
The fastest car in the world can travel at 393 miles per hour. It has a rocket engine to speed it along.

spark plug

piston

cylinder

connects to gears (see page 8)

crankshaft

fan belt drives the generator (see page 18)

A four-cylinder engine

The Gears

- Most cars have four or five gears. They help the car to travel at different speeds.

- Some gears are for starting off and driving slowly. Others are for driving fast or reversing (going backward).

- The gears are made up of lots of toothed wheels fixed to rods, or shafts.

- When two gear-wheels touch, the teeth fit together and one wheel turns the other.

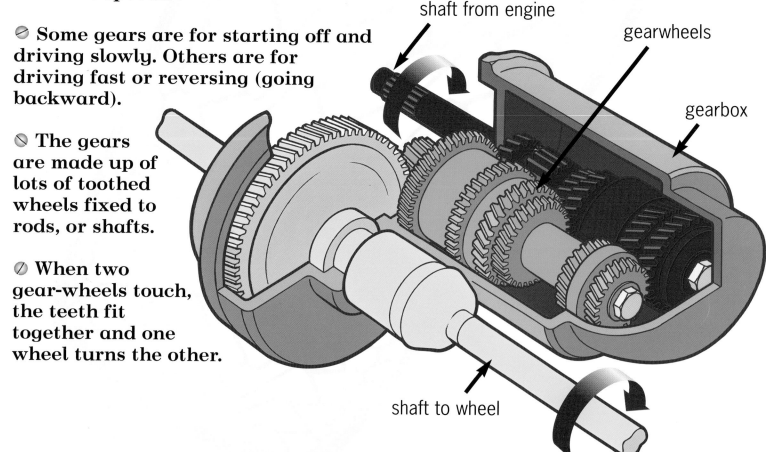

shaft from engine

gearwheels

gearbox

shaft to wheel

8

Fast and slow

The gearwheels are different sizes. Big gearwheels turn the shaft to the wheels faster than small gearwheels.

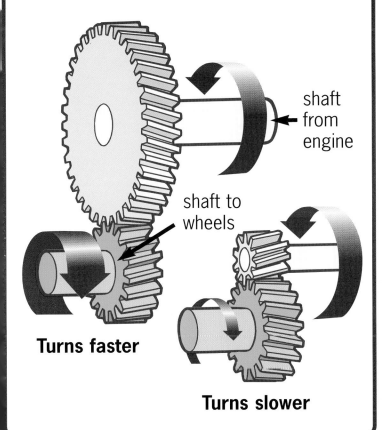

shaft from engine

shaft to wheels

Turns faster

Turns slower

Changing gear

In some cars, the gears change automatically. The gearshift is used for driving forward (D), reversing (R), and parking (P). N is for neutral, meaning no gear.

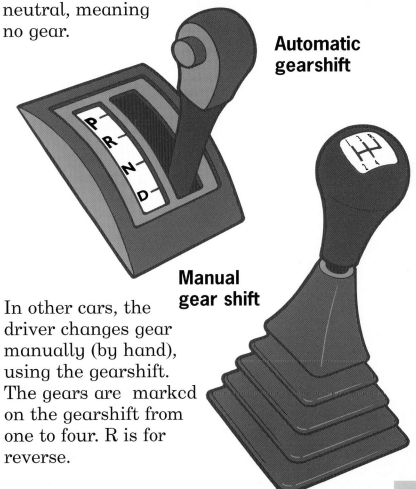

Automatic gearshift

Manual gear shift

In other cars, the driver changes gear manually (by hand), using the gearshift. The gears are marked on the gearshift from one to four. R is for reverse.

The Fuel System

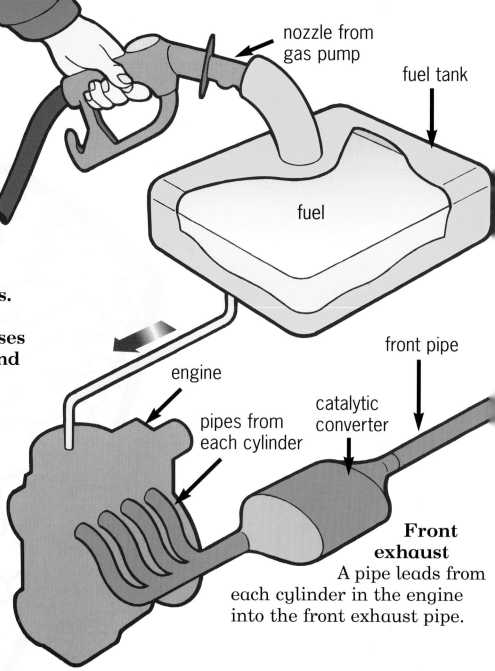

nozzle from gas pump

fuel tank

fuel

⊘ **Fuel for the engine is stored in the fuel tank.**

⊘ **When fuel explodes in the engine, it makes waste gases.**

◐ **The waste, or exhaust, gases go along the exhaust pipe and out of the car into the air.**

engine

front pipe

catalytic converter

pipes from each cylinder

Fact Box
Some large cars have such big, powerful engines that they need two or more exhaust pipes to get rid of all the waste gases.

Front exhaust
A pipe leads from each cylinder in the engine into the front exhaust pipe.

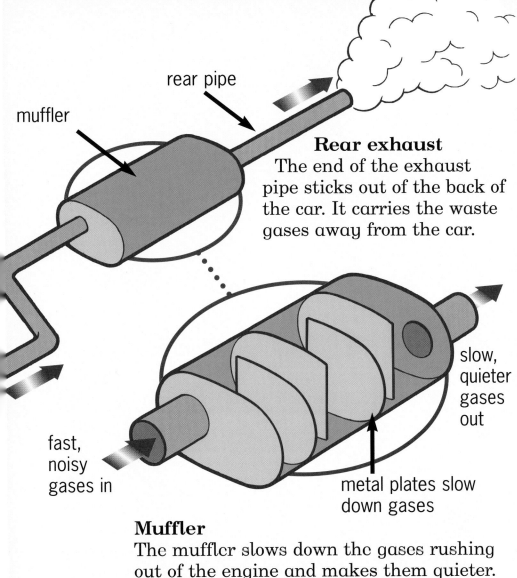

muffler

rear pipe

Rear exhaust
The end of the exhaust pipe sticks out of the back of the car. It carries the waste gases away from the car.

slow, quieter gases out

fast, noisy gases in

metal plates slow down gases

Muffler
The muffler slows down the gases rushing out of the engine and makes them quieter. Without a muffler, the escaping waste gases would be very noisy.

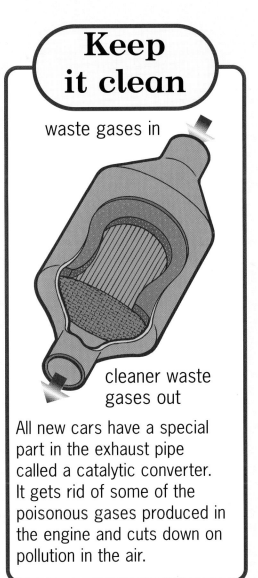

Keep it clean

waste gases in

cleaner waste gases out

All new cars have a special part in the exhaust pipe called a catalytic converter. It gets rid of some of the poisonous gases produced in the engine and cuts down on pollution in the air.

Wheels and Tires

⊘ **Most cars have four wheels, two at the front and two at the back.**

⊘ **The wheels are covered with tires, which help to grip the road and give a smooth ride.**

⊘ **The tires are lined with layers of thick fabric to make them strong.**

Fact Box
Wheels were invented more than 5,000 years ago. The first wheels were of solid wood.

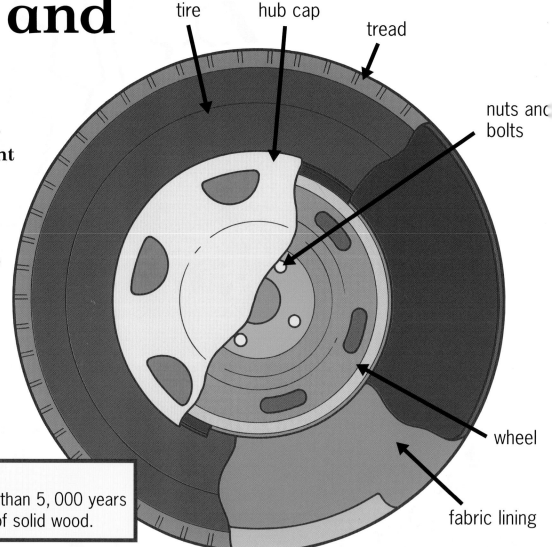

tire

hub cap

tread

nuts and bolts

wheel

fabric lining

Parts of a wheel

Hub cap
The hub cap covers the nuts and bolts that attach the wheel to the car.

Tire
The tire is made of rubber and filled with air. It is the only part of the car to touch the ground.

Wheel
The wheel rim holds the tire in place. It is made of steel or aluminum.

Shock absorber
A shock absorber lets the wheel move up and down slightly. This gives a smooth ride on bumpy roads.

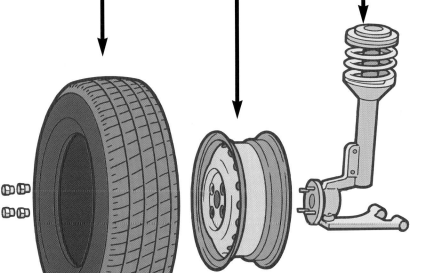

Tread carefully!
The patterns on tires are called treads. They help the car to grip the road in wet weather.

The Brakes

◎ Brakes are used to slow down the car and make it stop.

◎ Each wheel has its own brake. The front wheels have disc brakes, and the back wheels usually have drum brakes.

◎ The driver presses the brake pedal to put on the brakes.

◎ The brake pedal is connected to the brakes by tubing filled with a liquid called brake fluid.

Fact Box
Racing car brakes get so hot that they glow red. Cool air is pumped around them to stop them from melting.

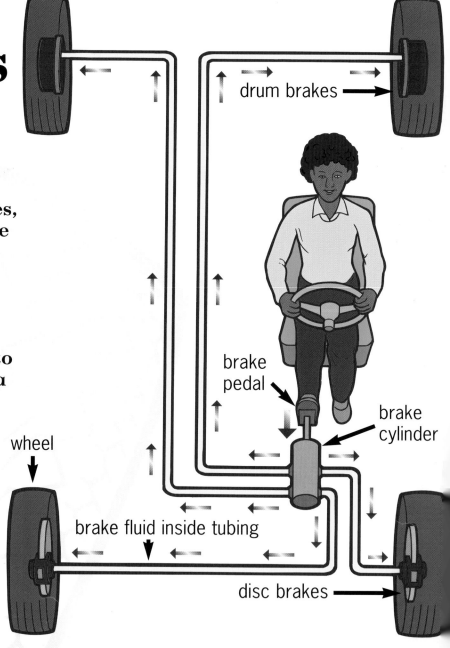

drum brakes

brake pedal

brake cylinder

wheel

brake fluid inside tubing

disc brakes

Putting on the brakes

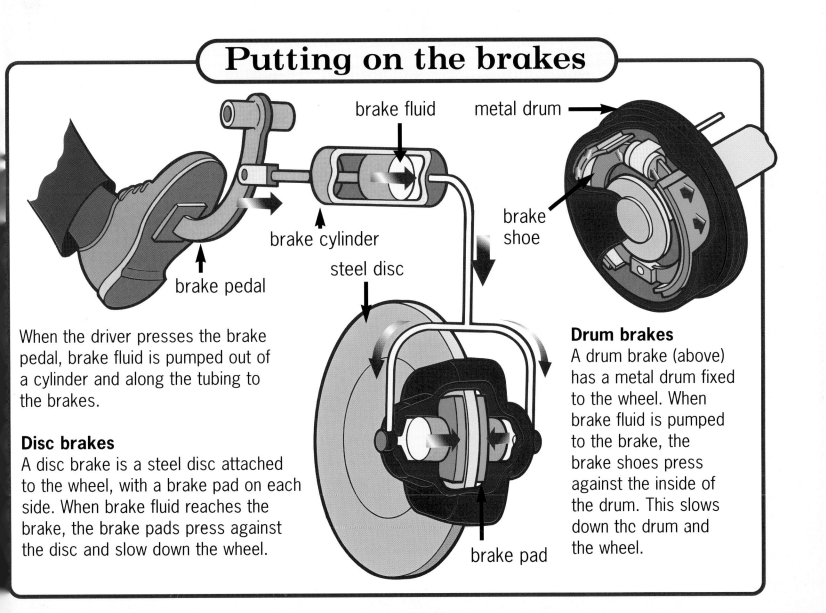

brake fluid

metal drum

brake cylinder

steel disc

brake shoe

brake pedal

brake pad

When the driver presses the brake pedal, brake fluid is pumped out of a cylinder and along the tubing to the brakes.

Disc brakes

A disc brake is a steel disc attached to the wheel, with a brake pad on each side. When brake fluid reaches the brake, the brake pads press against the disc and slow down the wheel.

Drum brakes

A drum brake (above) has a metal drum fixed to the wheel. When brake fluid is pumped to the brake, the brake shoes press against the inside of the drum. This slows down the drum and the wheel.

15

Steering

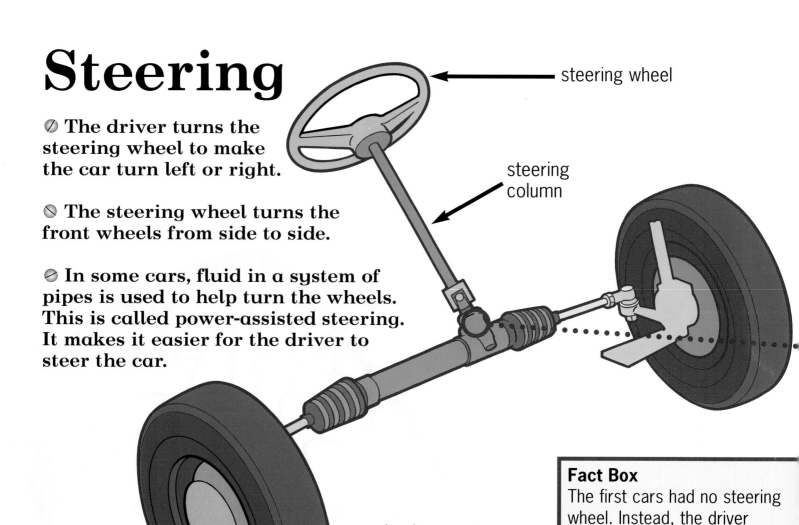

○ The driver turns the steering wheel to make the car turn left or right.

○ The steering wheel turns the front wheels from side to side.

○ In some cars, fluid in a system of pipes is used to help turn the wheels. This is called power-assisted steering. It makes it easier for the driver to steer the car.

steering wheel

steering column

wheel

Fact Box
The first cars had no steering wheel. Instead, the driver steered by moving a wooden stick, called a tiller, from side to side.

16

How the steering works

Steering column

The steering wheel is joined to the top of the steering column. When the driver turns the wheel, the steering column turns too.

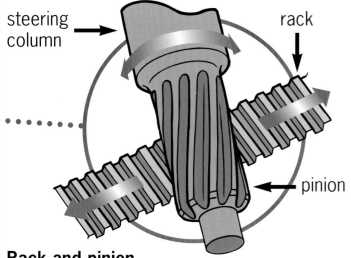

steering column

rack

pinion

Rack and pinion

At the bottom of the steering column is a gear-wheel called a pinion. When it turns, it makes a long bar, called a rack, move from side to side. This makes the wheels turn.

Turning left

When the steering wheel is turned to the left, the rack moves to the right and turns the front wheels to the left.

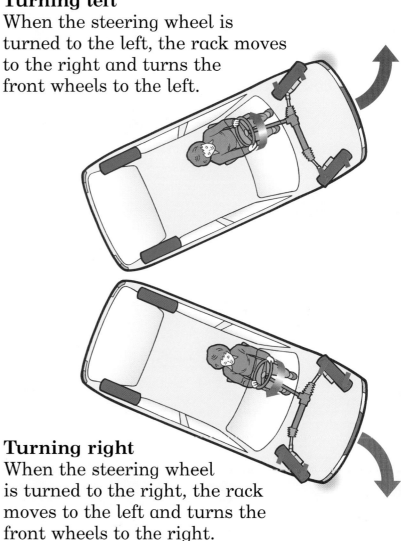

Turning right

When the steering wheel is turned to the right, the rack moves to the left and turns the front wheels to the right.

Lights and Electrical Systems

◉ **A car has four main groups of lights, two groups at the front and two at the back.**

◉ **The lights are powered by electricity from a machine called a generator.**

◉ **Electricity is also used to power the spark plugs, radio, heater, air conditioner, and wipers.**

Making electricity

Generator
When the engine is running (turned on), it turns around the generator. As it spins, the generator makes electricity.

Battery
When the engine is turned off, electricity for the lights comes from the battery. The battery is recharged by the generator.

Parts of a headlight

reflector gathers light from bulb into a narrow beam

bulb produces light

lens shines beam in the right direction

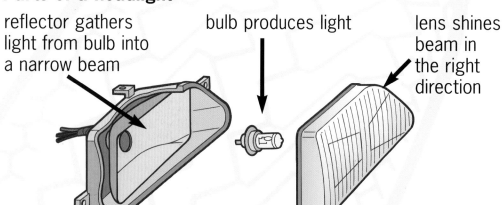

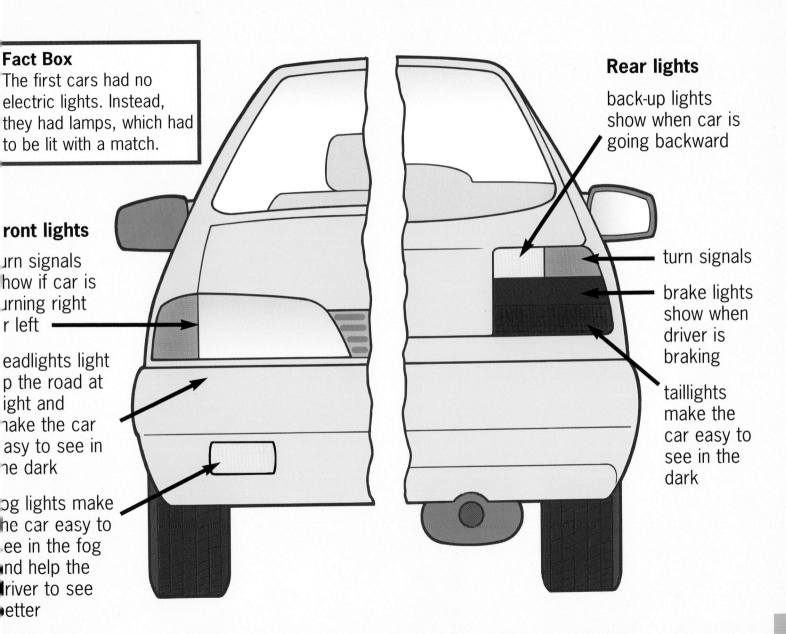

Front lights

turn signals show if car is turning right or left

headlights light up the road at night and make the car easy to see in the dark

fog lights make the car easy to see in the fog and help the driver to see better

Rear lights

back-up lights show when car is going backward

turn signals

brake lights show when driver is braking

taillights make the car easy to see in the dark

Inside the Car

⊘ There are comfortable seats inside the car, firmly attached to the floor.

⊘ The seats can be adjusted to suit tall or short people.

⊘ Mirrors are placed to let the driver see what is behind him or her on the road.

⊘ Seat belts, headrests, and sometimes air bags are installed to keep the driver and passengers safe in an accident.

Mirrors
The driver looks in a mirror above the windshield to see what is behind him or her on the road. Side-view mirrors on the outside give a wider view.

Handles and armrests
On the inside of the doors, there are handles to open and close the doors and windows, plus an armrest to lean on.

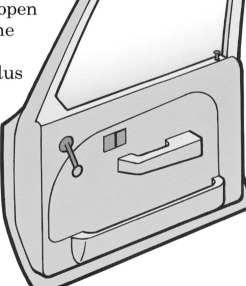

Carpets and covers
There is carpet on the floor and soft fabric covering the seats. In expensive cars, the seats may be covered in leather.

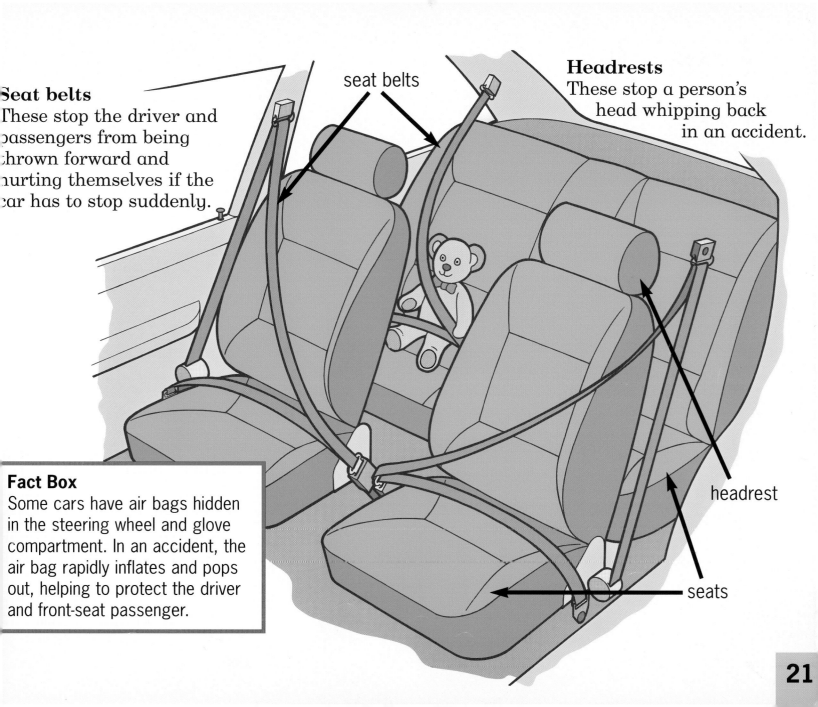

Seat belts
These stop the driver and passengers from being thrown forward and hurting themselves if the car has to stop suddenly.

seat belts

Headrests
These stop a person's head whipping back in an accident.

headrest

Fact Box
Some cars have air bags hidden in the steering wheel and glove compartment. In an accident, the air bag rapidly inflates and pops out, helping to protect the driver and front-seat passenger.

seats

The Dashboard

● The dashboard is a display of lights, measuring instruments, and switches.

● Measuring instruments, or gauges, give the driver information about the car.

● One set of switches controls the heating and air conditioning inside the car.

● Warning lights come on to warn the driver if something is wrong.

● There are also switches on the steering column to control the lights, turn signals, and windshield wipers.

Fact Box
Some modern cars have speaking dashboards. They tell people to fasten their seat belt and close their door properly.

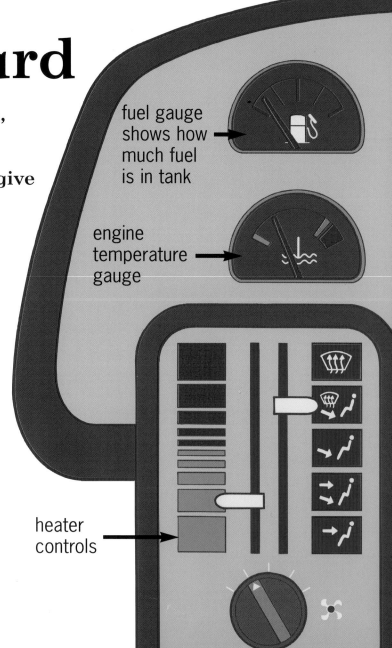

fuel gauge shows how much fuel is in tank

engine temperature gauge

heater controls

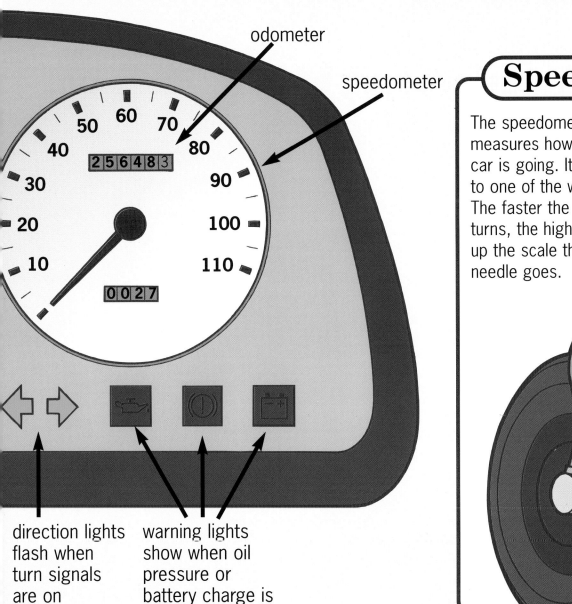

odometer

speedometer

50 60 70

40 80

256483

30 90

20 100

10 110

0027

direction lights flash when turn signals are on

warning lights show when oil pressure or battery charge is low or when brakes are worn

Speedometer

The speedometer measures how fast the car is going. It is attached to one of the wheels. The faster the wheel turns, the higher up the scale the needle goes.

scale

needle

wheel

The Body

The outside of a car is called the body.

⊘ All the other parts of the car are attached to the body.

◔ The body is usually made of steel, which is very strong. It is sprayed ◔ with several layers of special paint, which stops it from rusting.

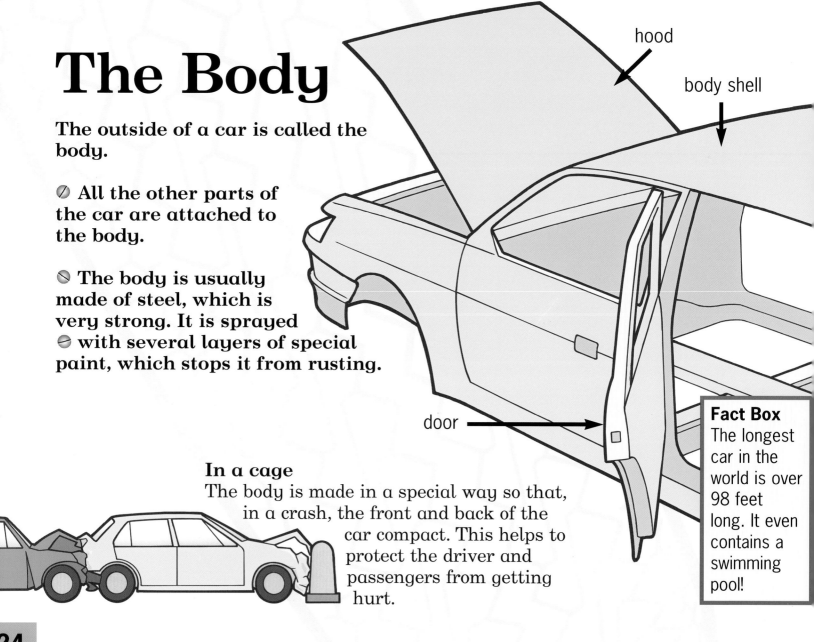

hood

body shell

door

In a cage
The body is made in a special way so that, in a crash, the front and back of the car compact. This helps to protect the driver and passengers from getting hurt.

Fact Box
The longest car in the world is over 98 feet long. It even contains a swimming pool!

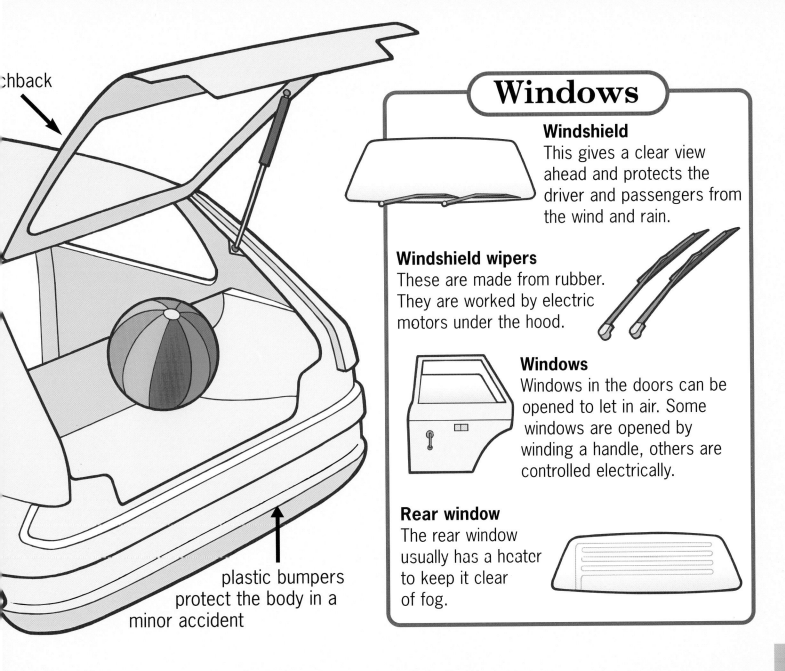

chback

plastic bumpers
protect the body in a
minor accident

Windows

Windshield
This gives a clear view ahead and protects the driver and passengers from the wind and rain.

Windshield wipers
These are made from rubber. They are worked by electric motors under the hood.

Windows
Windows in the doors can be opened to let in air. Some windows are opened by winding a handle, others are controlled electrically.

Rear window
The rear window usually has a heater to keep it clear of fog.

How a Car is Built

- Cars are made on a production line in a factory.

- Different parts are attached as the car moves along the production line.

- Some of the jobs on the line are done by robots.

- Some parts, such as the engine, are made on their own production line before being attached to the car.

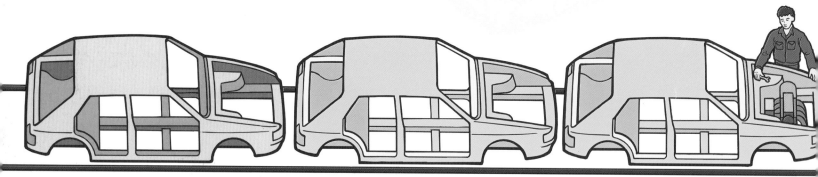

Making the body
Metal sheets are pressed into shape and welded together to form the body.

Painting the body
The body is dipped into a huge bath of chemicals to prevent rusting. Then it is painted.

Adding the engine
The engine is put in the hood and attached into place. Other parts are also added.

Robots

Unlike people, robots can do the same job again and again, without getting bored or tired. On car production lines, they do the paint spraying, welding, and lifting.

Doors and hood

The doors and hood are painted separately. Then they are attached to the body.

Scats and fittings

The carpets and seats, door handles, seat belts, and air bags are added next.

Finishing off

Finally, the windows and wheels are added. Then the car is driven off to be tested.

Special Parts

⊘ **Some cars are built for special jobs.**

◐ **They have different parts from normal cars.**

◑ **You can see some of these special parts on this spread.**

Flashing lights

Emergency vehicles, such as police cars a[n]
ambulances, have flashing lights on the
roof to warn other drivers to clear the roa[d]

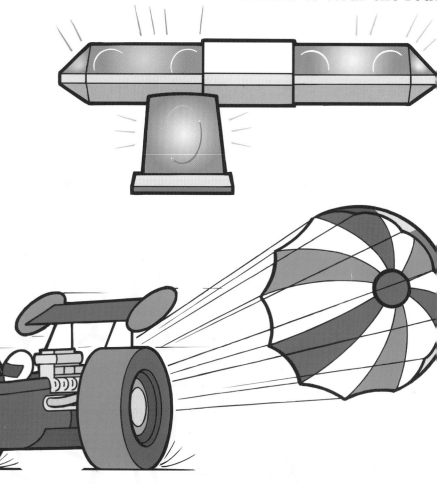

Parachutes

Drag-racing cars, or dragsters,
go so fast that they need a
parachute to help slow
them down again.

Wings

Racing cars have a winglike shape in the rear. This pushes the back of the car down so that the car grips the road better when it is going fast.

Roll bars

Rally cars have bars inside them that protect the driver and codriver if the car rolls over.

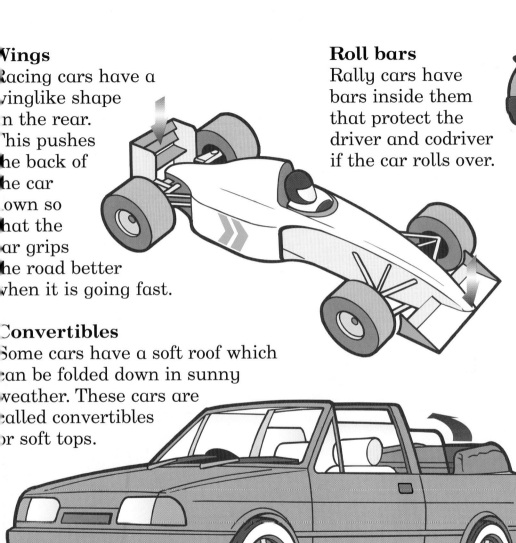

Convertibles

Some cars have a soft roof which can be folded down in sunny weather. These cars are called convertibles or soft tops.

Wheelchair lift

Cars can be fitted with a special mechanism that lifts a wheelchair and its passenger into the car. The wheelchair then locks firmly in place and acts as a car seat.

Useful Terms

air bag A large plastic bag, like a balloon, that inflates (blows up) very quickly in an accident to protect the driver or passenger from being thrown forward.

battery A device that stores electricity so that it can be used later.

bumper A piece of metal or plastic at the front or back of a car body that protects it from damage.

catalytic converter A metal box in the exhaust pipe that gets rid of some of the poisonous gases from the engine and helps to cut down pollution.

convertible A car with a roof that folds down so that the passengers are in the open air.

crankshaft The shaft turned by the pistons in a car's engine. It goes into the gearbox.

cylinder An opening in the engine—the shape of a soft drink can—where fuel burns. Pistons move up and down inside the cylinders. There are also cylinders in the brakes.

dashboard The panel of switches, lights, and dials in front of the driver.

disc brake A brake that slows down the car by forcing two pads against a metal disc fixed to the wheel.

drum brake A brake that slows down the car by pressing pads onto the inside of a metal drum fixed to the wheel.

exhaust A long pipe that takes waste gases from the engine and releases them into the air behind the car.

four-cylinder engine An engine with four cylinders. Some engines have six, eight, or even twelve cylinders to make them more powerful.

fuel A liquid that is burned inside the engine to make the engine work and the car move. It is stored in a fuel tank.

gears A set of gearwheels metal discs with teeth (around the rim) that lets the car go faster or slower, or forward or backward.

lights These are used to light up the road at night, let other drivers see the car, and to show when the car is turning or reversing. There are also warning lights on the dashboard.

muffler A metal box that is part of a car's exhaust pipe. It makes the engine much less noisy.

piston A piece of metal that moves up and down inside the cylinder of an engine. As it moves, it turns the engine's crankshaft.

power-assisted steering Steering that helps the driver to steer by making the steering wheel easier to turn.

production line The line of machines and workers in a factory along which a car moves as it is being built.

rocket engine An engine that works by shooting out a stream of hot gases. Rocket engines are normally used for missiles and spacecraft.

seat belt A long belt made of fabric that holds the driver and passengers in their seats. It stops them from being thrown about inside the car in a accident.

tire A rubber cover on the outside of a wheel. It helps the car grip the road, and makes the ride less bumpy.

turn signals Flashing lights at each corner of a car that tell other drivers which way the car is going to turn.

windshield The large window at the front of the car. It protects the driver and passengers from the wind and rain.

Index

air bag 20, 21, 30

battery 5, 18, 23, 30
body 5, 24, 25, 26
bolt 12, 13
brake 14, 15, 19, 23
brake fluid 14, 15
bumper 5, 25, 30

car factory 4, 26, 27
catalytic converter
  10, 11, 30
crankshaft 6, 7, 30
cylinder 6, 7, 10,
  14, 15, 30

dashboard 22, 30
door 5, 20, 24, 25, 27

electricity 6, 18
engine 5, 6, 7, 10,
  11, 18, 22, 26
exhaust 4, 10, 11, 30
exhaust gases 10, 11

fan belt 7
fuel 6, 10, 22, 31
fuel tank 10

gas 6
gas pedal 6
gearbox 8
gears 8, 9, 17, 31
gearwheels 5, 8, 9
generator 7, 18

hatchback 25
headrest 20, 21
heating 22, 25
hood 24, 26, 27
hub cap 12, 13

lights 5, 18, 19, 22,
  31

mirror 20
muffler 11, 31

odometer 23

pinion 17
piston 6, 7, 31
power-assisted
  steering 16, 31

rack 17
robot 26, 27
roll bars 29

seat 4, 20, 21, 27 29
seat belt 20, 21, 22,
  31
shock absorber 13
spark plug 6, 7, 18
speedometer 23

steering column 16,
  17, 22
steering wheel 4,
  16, 17, 21

tire 5, 12, 13, 31
tread 12, 13
turn signals 19, 22,
  23, 31

warning light 22,
  23, 28
wheel 5, 6, 12, 13,
  14, 15, 16, 17, 23, 27
wheelchair lift 29
window 5, 20, 25,
  27
windshield 5, 20,
  25, 31
windshield wipers
  18, 22, 25

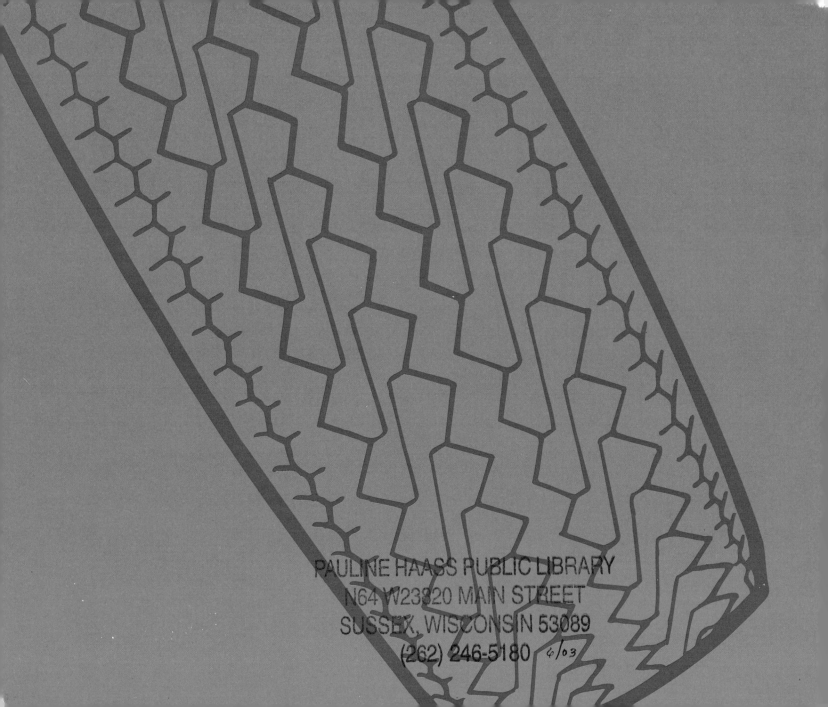